D0045103

We Need Dentists

by Lola M. Schaefer

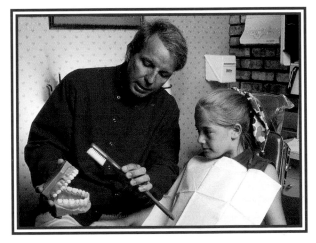

Consulting Editor: Gail Saunders-Smith, Ph.D.

Consultant: Isabel Garcia, D.D.S., M.P.H.
National Institute of Dental and Craniofacial Research

Pebble Books

an imprint of Capstone Press
Mankato, Minnesota

Pebble Books are published by Capstone Press
818 North Willow Street, Mankato, Minnesota 56001
http://www.capstone-press.com

Library of Congress Cataloging-in-Publication Data
Schaefer, Lola M., 1950–
    We need dentists/by Lola M. Schaefer.
    p. cm.—(Helpers in our community)
    Includes bibliographical references and index.
    Summary: Simple text and photographs present dentists and their role in
the community.
    ISBN 0-7368-0388-2
    1. Dentistry—Juvenile literature. 2. Dentists—Juvenile literature [1. Dentists
2. Dentistry. 3. Occupations.] I. Title. II. Series: Schaefer, Lola M., 1950– Helpers in
our community.
RK63.S297 2000
617.6—DC21
                                                                    99-19424
                                                                    CIP

Note to Parents and Teachers

The Helpers in Our Community series supports national social
studies standards for units related to community helpers and
their roles. This book describes and illustrates dentists and how
they help people. The photographs support early readers
in understanding the text. The repetition of words and phrases
helps early readers learn new words. This book also introduces
early readers to subject-specific vocabulary words, which are
defined in the Words to Know section. Early readers may need
assistance to read some words and to use the Table of Contents,
Words to Know, Read More, Internet Sites, and Index/Word List
sections of the book.

Table of Contents

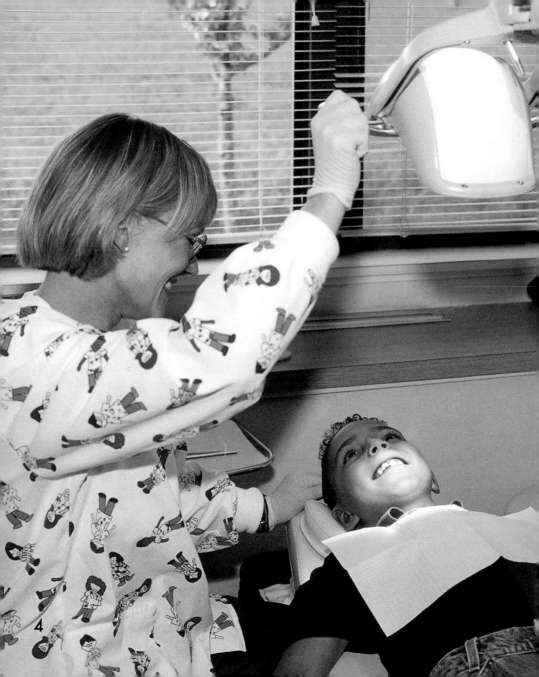

Dentists care
for people's mouths.

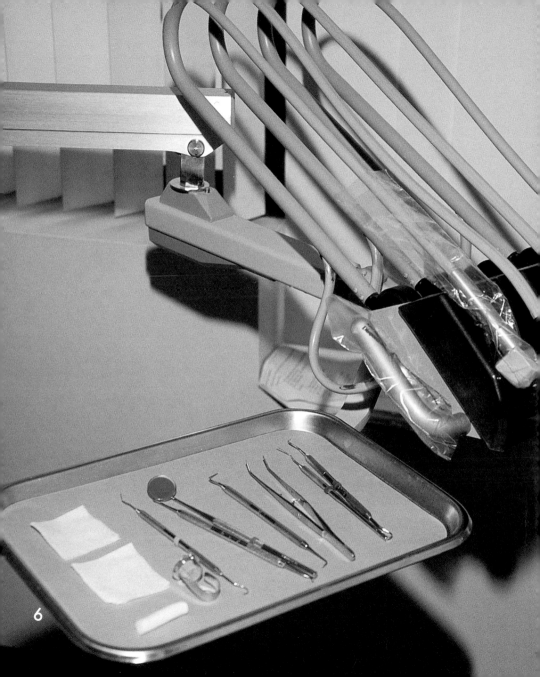

Dentists use special tools.

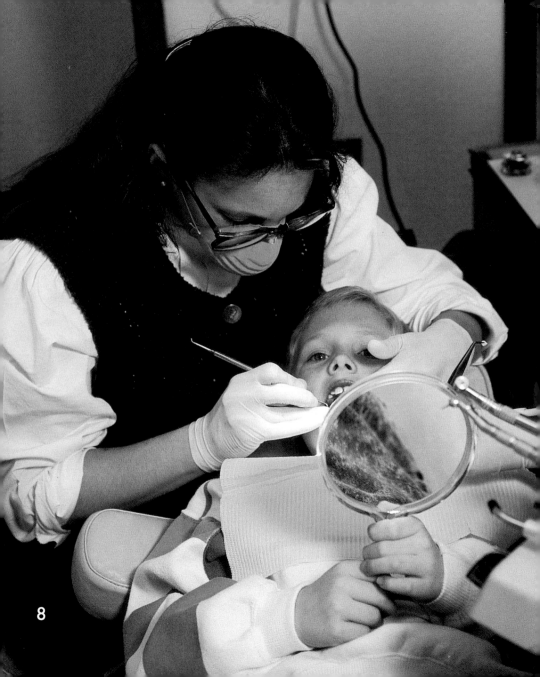

Dentists look at people's teeth and gums.

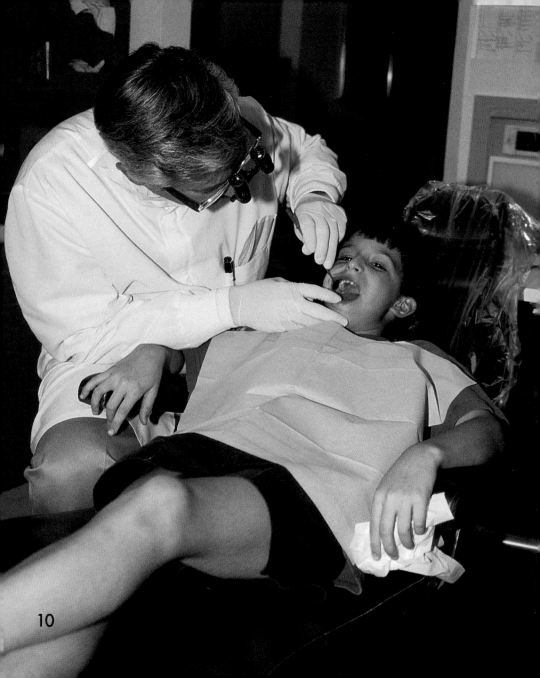

Dentists look at all parts of people's mouths.

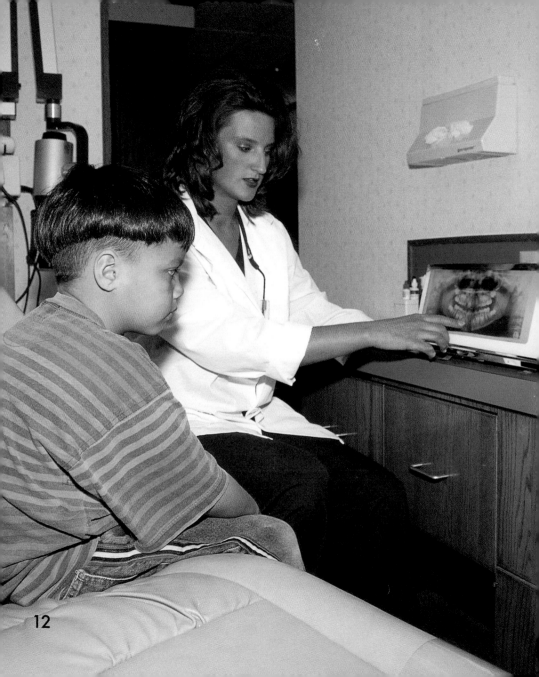

Dentists look at x-rays.

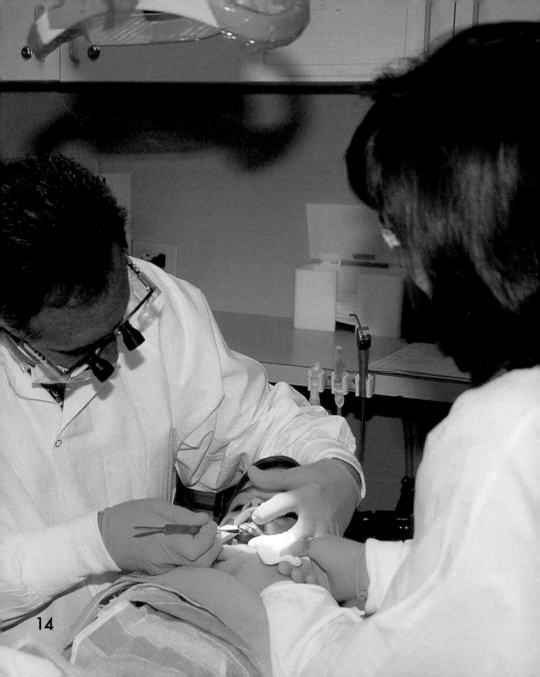

Dentists fix unhealthy teeth.

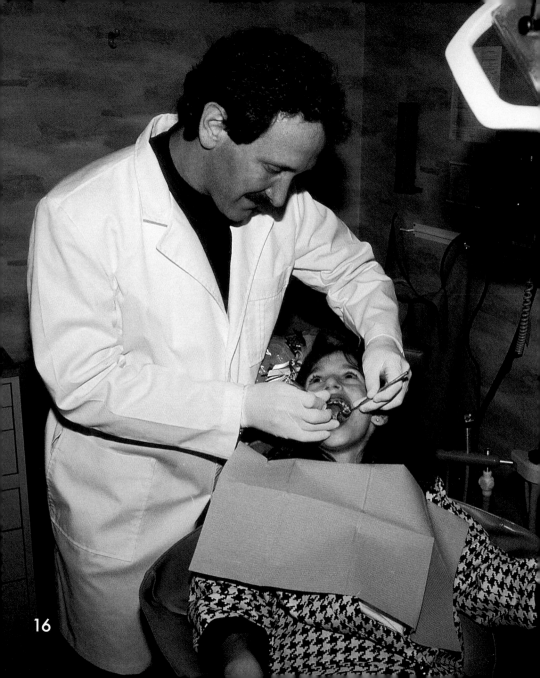

Some dentists attach braces to straighten teeth.

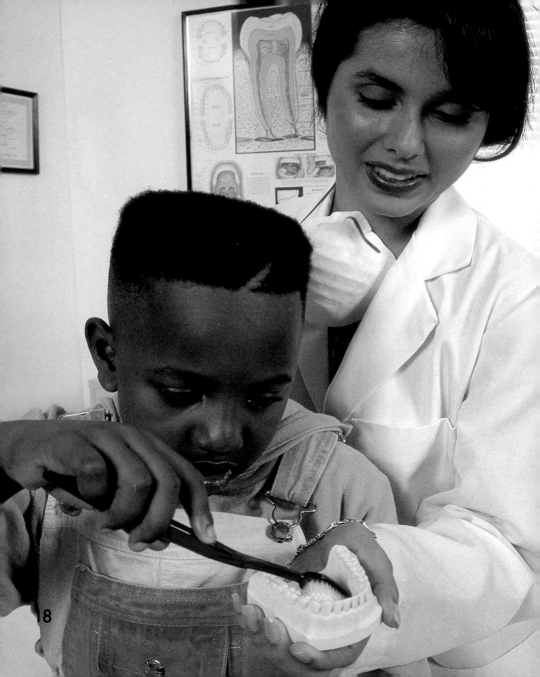

Dentists teach people how to care for their teeth.

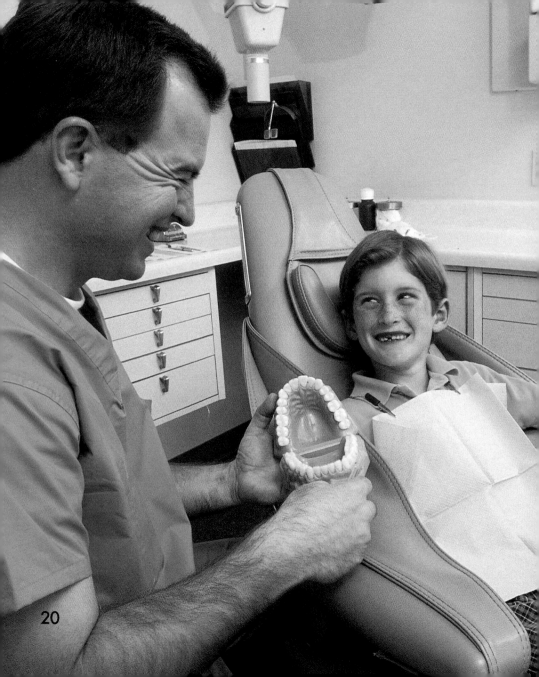

Dentists help keep people's mouths healthy.

Words to Know

attach—to join one thing to another; some dentists attach braces to teeth.

gums—the firm, pink skin at the base of teeth

healthy—fit and well; healthy teeth are strong, white, and work well.

straighten—to make straight; not bent; teeth that are not straight may not work right.

tool—an object used for a job; dentists use tools to examine, clean, polish, and repair teeth.

x-ray—a kind of photograph; dentists use x-rays to see if the inside of a person's mouth is healthy.

Read More

Frost, Helen. *Going to the Dentist.* Dental Health. Mankato, Minn.: Pebble Books, 1999.

Greene, Carol. *Dentists Take Care of Our Mouths.* Plymouth, Minn.: The Child's World, 1998.

Ready, Dee. *Dentists.* Community Helpers. Mankato, Minn.: Bridgestone Books, 1998.

Internet Sites

American Dental Association Kids' Corner
http://www.ada.org/consumer/kids/index.html

The Wisdom Tooth Homepage
http://www.umanitoba.ca/outreach/wisdomtooth

Wizard of the Magical Os
http://www.magicalos.com

Index/Word List

attach, 17
braces, 17
care, 5, 19
dentists, 5, 7, 9, 11,
   13, 15, 17, 19, 21
fix, 15
gums, 9
healthy, 21
help, 21
how, 19
keep, 21
look, 9, 11, 13

mouth, 5, 11, 21
parts, 11
people, 5, 9, 11,
   19, 21
some, 17
special, 7
straighten, 17
teach, 19
teeth, 9, 15, 17, 19
tools, 7
unhealthy, 15
x-rays, 13

Word Count: 54
Early-Intervention Level: 9

Editorial Credits
Karen L. Daas, editor; Abby Bradford, Bradfordesign, Inc., cover designer;
   Kimberly Danger, photo researcher

Photo Credits
David F. Clobes, 4, 12
Index Stock Imagery/Bill Bachmann, 1; Kent Vinyard, 8; Don B. Stevenson (1992), 20
Leslie O'Shaughnessy, 6
Photo Network/Tom McCarthy, 18
Ronald Cantor, 10, 14
Unicorn Stock Photos/Tom McCarthy, cover
Visuals Unlimited/Bernd Wittich, 16